HANS CHRISTIAN ANDERSEN

Mason Crest Publishers, Inc.
370 Reed Road
Broomall, Pennsylvania 19008
866-MCP-BOOK (toll free)

Illustrations copyright © 2001
Art Agency "PIART"
Published in association with
Grimm Press Ltd., Taiwan
Printed in Taiwan.
1 3 5 7 9 8 6 4 2

Library of Congress Cataloging-in-Publication Data:

on file at the Library of Congress.

ISBN 1-59084-160-3
ISBN 1-59084-133-6 (series)

Great Names

HANS CHRISTIAN ANDERSEN

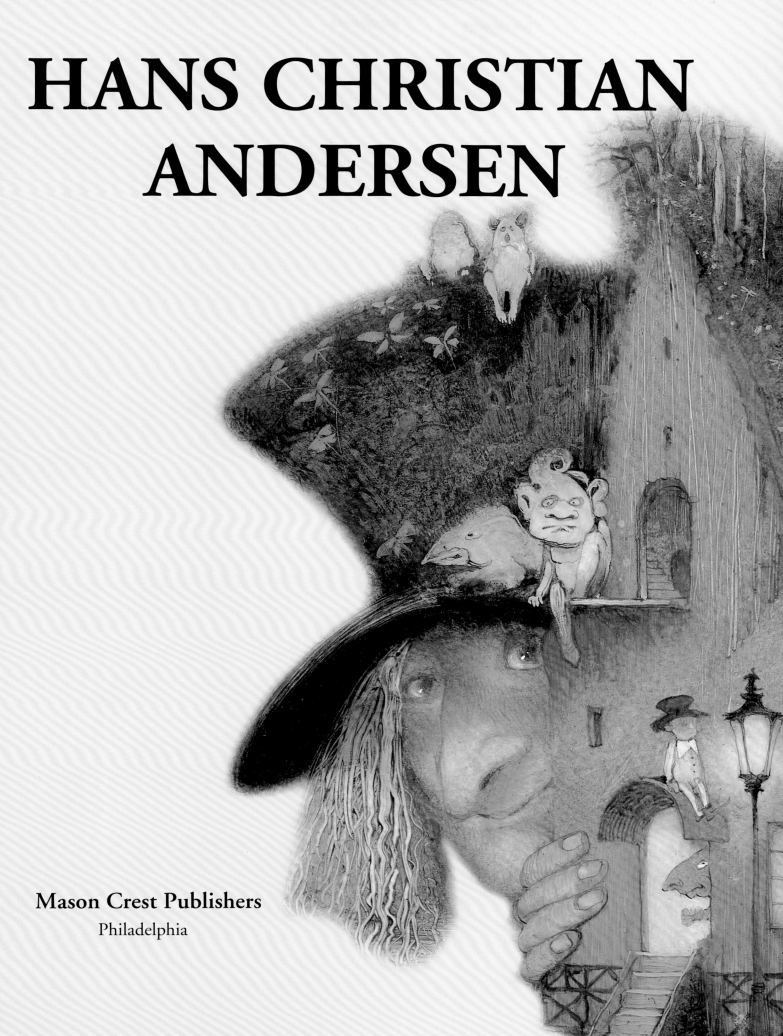

Mason Crest Publishers

Philadelphia

Little Hans Christian Andersen lifted his unhappy face and looked at his grandmother. "Why do I look different from other children? Why don't they like to do the things that I like to do?"

"Because you're the best boy in the world, and some day, you will become a great man." Hans was his grandmother's favorite. Although they did not live together, she walked a great distance to see him every day.

Hans did look different. He had small eyes on either side of a big nose and long thin legs, like a stork. The neighbor children called him "scarecrow." When he walked, his legs wobbled, and he often fell down. Everything about him was clumsy, like an ugly duckling.

Hans Christian Andersen was born in 1805 in the town of Odense, near Copenhagen in Denmark. His father was a poor shoemaker, and his mother was a washerwoman.

To make ends meet, the family lived in a single, small room. Even though they barely had enough food to eat or clothes to wear, Hans's father loved him dearly. He would sit by his son's bed every night before bedtime

and read him adventures from *The Arabian Nights' Entertainments*. These stories fascinated little Hans, helping him forget life's real troubles. He would imagine that Aladdin and Sinbad the Sailor had stepped out of the book and invited him onto a magic carpet for a journey to mystical Arabia.

"Andersen the Freak" was another mean nickname young Hans endured. He never played with the other boys, but sat by himself in a corner of his house, mumbling stories to himself. Although he didn't like going to school, Hans loved books. As soon as he got his hands on a new book, he would quickly read it from cover to cover.

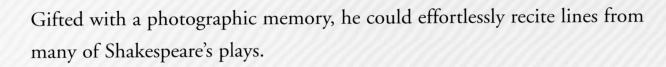

Gifted with a photographic memory, he could effortlessly recite lines from many of Shakespeare's plays.

Andersen's father made seven wooden figurines for him. Hans would imagine himself as the king of the castle and pretend his wooden figurines were his subjects: the queen, prince, princess, general, soldier, clown, and beggar. They would follow him in his wars against the enemy and in his quest for treasure. Hans would come up with new stories for his figurines every day. Even as a young boy, his mind was full of tales of adventure and glory.

When he was seven, Hans went to his first performance of a play. He was spellbound by the actors.

They were far more interesting than his stiff wooden figurines because they could talk, sing, dance, and even turn somersaults. It was a wonderful day for the boy. With that first performance, he fell in love with the theater. To him, the stage seemed like some sort of glorious paradise. He decided then that he would become an actor. What young Hans did not understand was how remote such a dream was for him. In the 19th century, the theater in Denmark was part of the world of the rich and powerful. A poor boy like him could only gaze at it from afar.

When Hans was 11 years old, his father died, and so he lost his dearest friend. He began to write plays as a way to comfort himself. His enthusiasm for the theater was matched only by his need for an approving audience. When he finished a play, he would knock on the doors of his neighbors, looking for someone who would listen and who loved the theater the way he did.

The neighbors thought that he was crazy, as he tried to act out the plays he had written on their doorsteps. They told his mother that she should try to find work for him, something more useful than performing his strange stories.

But Hans adored the theater. He told his mother, "Some day, I will be great. I'm not afraid of hardship, if that's what it takes to be famous."

His mother was very poor. She would have liked Hans to help her by earning some money. But she kept in mind her husband's dying words: "Let the child do whatever he would like, as long as it makes him happy."

Hans had a beautiful voice. By the side of the Odense River, there was a large flat rock, which his mother used as a washboard. But Hans imagined that it was a marvelous stage. Standing on this rock, he would loudly sing songs he had written. He hoped his beautiful voice would let him into the world of the theater.

After a while, people began to talk about the talented boy, who sang by the river. They invited Hans to perform for them. One day, the Prince of Odense asked Hans to come and sing for him. The boy was overwhelmed by the honor. He sang one sweet song after another for the Prince, who nodded with approval.

When Hans finished singing, the Prince asked him what he wanted to do next. Hans didn't hesitate for a moment. "I want to be an actor," he said.

The Prince frowned slightly. "An actor? You're a talented boy, but your family is so poor. Learning a skill would be much more realistic. If you decide to become something useful, like a carpenter or a tailor, I will help you."

But Hans would not change his mind, even for the Prince. "No, thank you. I don't want to do anything else. My dream is to perform on the stage of the Royal Theater in Copenhagen."

Without the help of someone rich or powerful, there was no future for Hans in Odense. So, like the ugly duckling leaving the nest, he set out to explore the wide world on his own. He arrived in Copenhagen when he was just 14 years old. When he saw the magnificent walls of the capital city, he wept with joy. Hans thought that his dream was about to come true. He had only 13 kroner in his pocket, but he was not discouraged. First, he found a place to live. Then he combed his hair and put on a clean shirt. He was ready to visit Madame Schall.

Madame Schall was the most famous dancer in the Royal Opera. Hans firmly believed that once Madame Schall watched him perform, she would give him a job. He planned to show her his "great somersault." To his dismay, just as he took off his boots to do his wonderful trick, Madame Schall stood up and impatiently waved him away.

Unable to hide his disappointment, Hans cried as he put on his boots and prepared to go. Watching the tears roll down the boy's cheeks, Madame Schall took pity on him. She sent him to talk to the director of the theater.

The director took one look at Hans and shook his head. "How could such a scrawny fellow be an actor?" The innocent Hans replied, "If you hire me, then I will have enough money to fatten up."

No one wanted Hans as a performer, but he didn't give up. He saw himself as an ugly duckling, hidden in the weeds. But he dreamed of the day when he would be transformed into a beautiful swan, soaring among the clouds.

One day, Hans read about the choirmaster, Giuseppe Siboni, in the newspaper. "I have a good voice," he thought. "Perhaps he'll give me a job." Hans gathered up his courage and rang Siboni's doorbell.

When Siboni first set eyes on Hans, he thought, "How can such an odd-looking fellow have any talent?" Although he was in the middle of a dinner party, Siboni gave in to Hans's pleas for an audition. Accompanied by the flowing notes of a piano, Hans sang of his hopes and dreams, with a voice as clear and sweet as a running brook. When he finished singing, Siboni's guests stood up and clapped. "Encore! Encore!" they cheered.

"My son, you sang very well. I will be your teacher," said Siboni, smiling at Hans.

"Sir, do you really mean it?" Hans pinched himself, hardly daring to believe his good luck.

But his good luck did not last long. Copenhagan's wet winter made Hans ill, and a racking cough hurt his vocal chords. Even worse, the boy was becoming a man, and his beautiful voice was changing. Siboni did not want Hans as a student any longer. The choirmaster suggested that Hans return to Odense. But this was impossible for him. He couldn't abandon his dream of standing on stage, listening to the applause of the audience. He knew he couldn't go home yet.

He didn't know what to do or where to turn next. Just when he was ready to give up, a friend found him a small part in a ballet performance. It was just a walk-on role, but it put "Hans Christian Andersen" on a playbill for the first time. Hans carried the playbill with him everywhere, taking it out every now and then to smile foolishly at his printed name. Every night before going to bed, he would study the playbill in the candlelight. These were happy days for the young man.

But these happy days weren't meant to last. Within three months, Andersen had lost his job at the theater. The director dismissed him with these heartless words: "You will never be anything more than a bit player."

Andersen was hurt by the cruel comment of the director, but it gave him a wonderful idea. He thought, "Perhaps I have failed as a performer,

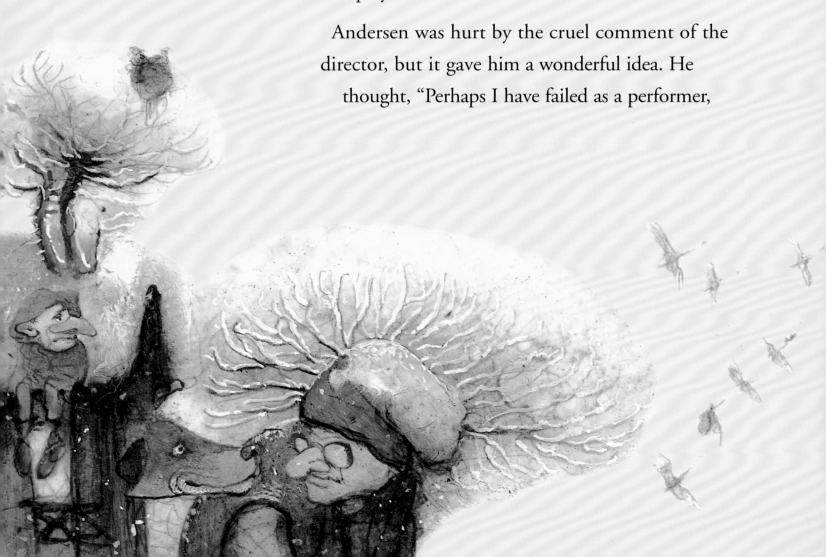

but that doesn't mean I have failed at the theater. I can write plays." He shook off his old disappointments and eagerly looked toward the future: "They don't like my appearance but they might like what's in my head. My writing could be the key that finally opens the door of the Royal Theater."

Even though Andersen had a head full of stories, he had little education. His vocabulary was poor, and he could hardly spell. His first play was immediately sent back to him. But Andersen just shrugged and started on a second. He read what he wrote to whomever would listen and begged for advice. Only when he had encouraging comments from his tenth listener did he dare to send his work to the director of the Royal Theater.

Once again, Andersen was met with disappointment. He waited an entire summer without receiving a response. He was so poor that he barely had enough food. His clothes were so old that he had outgrown them. His shirtsleeves reached his elbows, and his trousers barely covered his legs. Just when he had no hope left, a savior named Jonas Collin entered his life.

Mr. Collin was one of the directors of the Royal Theater in Copenhagen. He admired the fresh ideas in Andersen's plays and believed that with more education, the young man could become a good writer.

"Would you like to return to school and continue your studies?" Mr. Collin asked kindly.

"Yes, I would," said Andersen eagerly, "but I don't even have enough money to feed myself. Where would I get the money for school?"

"Don't worry," replied Mr. Collin. "I have found a scholarship for you that will allow you to go to school for three years, free of charge."

At first, Andersen thought he had misunderstood Mr. Collin. Three years of free schooling! He didn't realize then how much school would help him. But the thought of free room and board for three years made Andersen smile, even in his sleep.

Yet life in school would not be easy.

Because Andersen had received so little education, he was placed in a class with 12-year-old boys, even though he was 17. He towered over his classmates, but he knew much less than they did. Even so, Andersen was eager to learn. He hadn't realized that the world was so full of interesting things. Like a sponge soaking up water,

he eagerly absorbed whatever he was taught. He never took time off, even during vacations. School would have been wonderful, if it weren't for the headmaster, Simon Meisling.

Simon Meisling was a round man with a fierce temper. He took it out on his students whenever he felt like it. He picked on Andersen the most, since he thought the young man was poor and had no right to a fine education. In Denmark at that time, there were strict distinctions among the social

classes. Only upper-class children had the privilege of studying in good schools. Meisling often scolded Andersen in front of the entire class. He would say things like, "You're an idiot. I have never seen such a stupid, lazy fellow." If the insults caused Andersen's eyes to fill with tears, Meisling would point to him and say, "Look at you, you great big crybaby."

No matter what he did, Andersen could not avoid the abuse of Headmaster Meisling. Not only would Meisling insult Andersen, but also he would order him to do the work of servants, such as cleaning up and looking after Meisling's children. Meisling even tore up poems that Andersen had carefully written. Such treatment filled the young man with despair. For years, even after he'd left school, Andersen dreamed of being beaten and cursed by this headmaster.

Once again, the ugly duckling struggled to dodge the hardships and cruelty that came his way.

After three years of studying in Meisling's school, Andersen felt like a tightly wound cord. The constant worry had made him as thin and weak as a scarecrow. But he couldn't rest, as he needed to pass his college entrance exams. So he buckled down to study once more, passing his exams and becoming a student at the University of Copenhagen in 1828. On his first day of classes at the University, Andersen was so excited that he shouted at the top of his lungs, "I'm a college student now!" He could now choose to become a doctor, a lawyer, or a minister. But his first choice was to become a writer.

Andersen's friends often saw him bent over a small wooden desk, writing furiously. His face was unshaven and his hair uncombed, but it didn't matter. In those moments, he was king of his castle of words, dictating the twists and turns of a story. The hand holding the pen was full of power, commanding each word to fall into place. "Writing is great fun," Andersen told his friends. He did not know then that one day he would command the attention of the world with his pen.

When he was still in college, one of Andersen's plays was performed in the Royal Theater. On opening night, his schoolmates cheered loudly, "Long live Andersen!" But Andersen was silent, watching the characters he'd created come to life on stage. His eyes filled with tears of joy. Even though he never fulfilled his childhood dream of performing on stage, he had, indeed, become a man of the theater. It had been a long journey, but he finally realized his dream.

As happy as this made him, Andersen was searching for more: he wanted to find someone to love. Riborg Voigt, a sister of a friend, was

Andersen's first love. Under the stars, they strolled through gardens and talked about poetry. Andersen thought he had finally found a true companion. Riborg understood Andersen and admired his writing, but she became engaged to another man. Andersen was heartbroken.

Around the same time, critics started finding fault with Andersen's writing. Some even read his poems for the sake of counting errors and ridiculing him for enjoyment. These attacks made Andersen feel terrible. He began to doubt himself and his dreams. During this difficult time, Louise, the youngest daughter of Jonas Collin, gave him her sympathy and support. Gradually, Andersen began to feel very fond of this young woman he had known since her girlhood. But she, too, became engaged to another man. Andersen felt miserable and wondered if the ugly duckling would ever receive his share of happiness. In despair, he wished he could leave Copenhagen, the critics, and his broken heart behind.

It wasn't long before he had his wish. In 1833, the Danish government awarded Andersen a scholarship for young artists. This allowed him to travel throughout Europe for two years. In the course of his travels, he wrote his first novel, *The Improvisatore* (1835). Before his novel was published, he finished working on his first collection of children's stories, called *Tales, Told for Children* (1835).

This collection had four tales: "The Tinderbox," "The Princess and the Pea," "Little Ida's Flowers," and "Big Claus and Little Claus." He wrote these stories just to make enough money to live on before his novel began to sell. At the time, Andersen had no idea that his children's stories would become the cornerstone of his success. He joked that they were "inconspicuous minor things."

Imagine Andersen's surprise when these stories made a stir in the literary world. Critics spread the news that a new literary star was born.

In their opinion, the children's tales were the best writing that Andersen had produced. But Andersen didn't agree. "They have it all wrong," he thought. "I'm prouder of my novels." Even so, he kept working on new children's stories.

One day, while Andersen was sitting on a sea wall watching the waves crash and surge below him, he had a sudden inspiration. He quickly took out a pen and paper and wrote the following words: "Down in the deepest depths of the sea there lived a little mermaid. Her eyes were of a deeper

blue than the color of the deepest sea." And so "The Little Mermaid" was born. This beloved tale, which became known throughout the world, had its beginnings on this sunny afternoon. This was also the moment when Andersen decided to devote himself to writing stories for children.

The more love Andersen gave to his children's stories, the more his young readers began to love him. They thought that Andersen had to be some sort of angel to create such wonderful tales. Whenever children saw Andersen, they would run up and hug him. He was like a magnet, attracting children with both his kind heart and storytelling talent. They didn't care if he wasn't handsome.

Inspired by his young readers' enthusiasm for his stories, Andersen wrote two more books for children. He was determined to use language that children could easily understand but not protect them from the harsh realities of life. The final words of his stories were never "and they lived happily ever after."

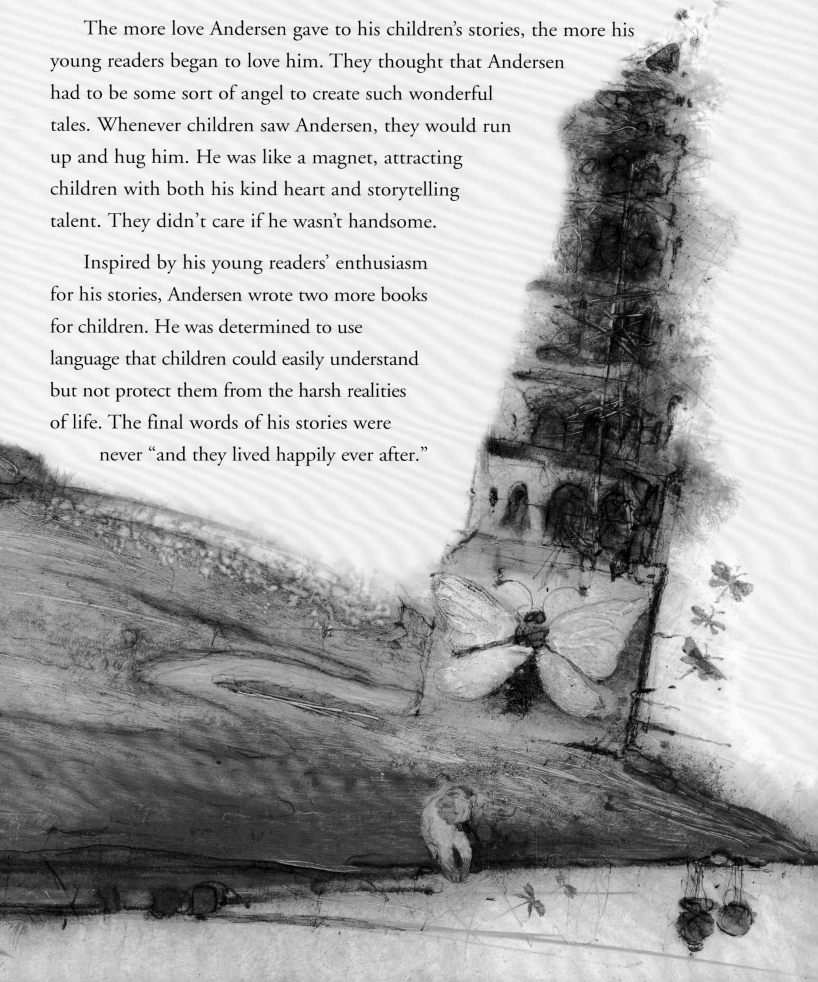

When the little mermaid wants to become human, she must give up her beautiful voice in return. The poor little match girl has to work hard just to stay alive. Andersen's stories show that nothing in the world is given freely.

In the early 19th century, Jacob and Wilhelm Grimm traveled around their home in Germany collecting fables, fairy tales, and folk stories. The brothers put these stories together in a famous book called *Grimm's Fairy Tales* (1812–22). Andersen's tales are different from these traditional fairy tales. Instead of retelling old stories, Andersen led his readers into the imaginary world he'd created. To him, everything great or small, wonderful or ordinary, had an amazing story to tell. He once wrote: "As I walk along the road, I see fences, streams, and butterflies beckoning to me. 'Wait a second,' they say, 'I have something to tell you.'"

Daisies swaying in the wind were beautiful princesses in disguise. Dragonflies flitting over the meadows were warriors. Fir trees moaned about becoming Christmas trees, their backs heavily burdened with too many decorations. In Andersen's mind, even ordinary little sewing needles could stand up to the five human fingers that deprived them of their freedom.

Andersen made a point of writing a tale every Christmas for children. Over the course of his lifetime, he wrote 164 children's stories. His name has come to mean good children's literature.

Most of Andersen's tales for children reflect something of his own experiences. He once said, "There is a shadow of me in every one of my tales."

As a child, Andersen had a lot in common with the ugly duckling of his tale. They were both excluded because they looked strange. To avoid being bullied, they often hid in lonely corners. They knew about the fear of being chased and the loneliness of being rejected.

Andersen spent his childhood as hungry as the little match girl, who imagined she saw a table covered with delicious food. The little match girl tried to sell matches in order to buy food with the money. Andersen went around trying to sell his talent, trying to feed both his stomach and his dreams.

And the silent little mermaid suffered as Andersen did, when he helplessly watched those he loved leave him, unable to find his voice to stop them.

With the success of his stories for children, Andersen became one of the most famous writers in all of Denmark. Gradually, the entire world came to know him and his work. Young Andersen had invented stories of kings and queens, princes and princesses. As an adult, these powerful people became his friends. It was as if his childhood dreams came true. Members of the nobility considered it an honor to invite Andersen into their mansions and castles. After dinner, they would gather around Andersen and beg him to tell his latest tale. Even after he became famous, Andersen hadn't completely changed. The ugly duckling had indeed become a swan, but he was still a quiet, humble man. He knew that people loved him for his stories, and he was grateful for the inspiration that gave him.

In Andersen's tale, the ugly duckling became a swan with a coat of beautiful white feathers. Only when the swan flew high into the clouds was it understood that he was no ordinary being. And so it was with Andersen.

In June 1867, Odense chose Andersen as its honorary citizen. On the day when Andersen was to be presented with the key to the city, banners flew everywhere, proclaiming, "Andersen Honors Odense." The streets were crowded with children and adults wanting to catch a glimpse of the famous citizen. They stood with his picture in their hands, waiting to welcome him.

That night, every home lit candles in their windows in his honor. Andersen looked out his window at Odense glittering with candlelight. How he wished his family could have been there with him, sharing the honor. It seemed like only yesterday when his mother told 14-year-old Hans, "A life of hardship comes before fame." How could 50 years have passed so quickly?

Andersen's stories have traveled the world and survived the test of time. Over the years, children and adults have loved his tales for their imaginative power. His stories didn't avoid showing cruelty or despair, but they are more about truth and goodness. Although Andersen never intended to be a teacher, his stories teach a lesson of the spirit: As long as you have a dream, you can write your own story, as rich, wonderful, and interesting as your imagination.

BIOGRAPHY

Author Anna Carew-Miller is a freelance writer and former teacher, who lives in rural northwestern Connecticut with her husband and daughter. Although she has a Ph.D. in American Literature and has done extensive research and writing on literary topics, most recently Anna has written books for younger children, including reference books and middle reader mysteries.